SOCCER'S
G.O.A.T.
MOMENTS

PUBLISHED FOR THE USA IN 2025 BY WELBECK CHILDREN'S BOOKS
An imprint of Hachette Children's Group
Part of Hodder & Stoughton Limited
Carmelite House, 50 Victoria Embankment, London, EC4Y 0DZ
An Hachette UK Company
www.hachette.co.uk
www.hachettechildrens.co.uk

An Hachette UK Company
www.hachette.co.uk
www.hachettechildrens.co.uk

DISCLAIMER
This book has not been authorized, licensed or endorsed by Fédération Internationale de Football Association (FIFA) or any associated company.

Active stats correct as of June 2025

10 9 8 7 6 5 4 3 2 1
ISBN 978 1 8045 3879 1

Printed and bound in China

Author: Kevin Pettman
Senior Commissioning Editor: Suhel Ahmed
Design Manager: Matt Drew
Picture research: Paul Langan
Production: Melanie Robertson
Consultant: Alex Rice

PICTURE CREDITS

The publishers would like to thank the following sources for their kind permission to reproduce the pictures in this book.

Alamy Stock Photo: Associated Press 16-17, 75; Frank Augstein/Associated Press 41T; Felipe Dana/Associated Press 12-13; diebilderwelt 33R; Isabel Infantes/PA Images 7, 14-15; 1010 Images 52B; Matt Jacques 110T; Sydney Low/Associated Press 110B; Sydney Low/Cal Sport Media 90-91; Daniel Motz 60, 89; Pressinphoto Sports Agency 32-33; Peter Robinson/PA Images 91T; Sipa US 109B; Xinhua 67T

Getty Images: AFP 8-9, 78-79; AMA/Corbis 96B, 106; Odd Andersen/AFP 38B, 39T; Archivo El Grafico 48B; The Asahi Shimbun 22-23; Mikoaj Barbanell/SOPA Images/LightRocket 37; Steve Bardens/FIFA 11T; Michel Barrault/Onze/Icon Sport 85TR; Paul Bereswill 48-49; Bettmann 74; Lionel Bonaventure/AFP 81; Gabriel Bouys/AFP 38-39; Jose Breton/Pics Action/NurPhoto 53R; Damian Briggs/Speed Media/Icon Sportswire 26-27; Simon Bruty /Sports Illustrated 10-11B; David Cannon /Allsport 111B; Philippe Caron/Sygma 103T; Central Press 65T; Yasuyoshi Chiba/AFP 99, 105; Tim Clayton/Corbis 15T; Mario De Biasi/Mondadori 62-63; Carl de Souza/AFP 108; Jacques Demarthon/AFP 112; Franck Fife/AFP 27B, 36, 52-53, 66-67, 70-71; Stuart Franklin/FIFA 10; Alain Gadoffre/Onze/Icon Sport 83; Daniel Garcia/AFP 28B; Paul Gilham 104; Georges Gobet/AFP 18-19; Laurence Griffiths 32B; Jack Guez/AFP 103B; Volker Hartmann/AFP 84; Ferdi Hartung/ullstein bild 50-51; Patrick Hertzog/AFP 86-87; Mike Hewitt/FIFA 73; Horstmüller/ullstein bild 31, 34, 63T; Philippe Huguen/AFP 101; Keystone-France/Gamma-Keystone 79T; Christof Koepsel/Bongarts 80; Ozan Kose/AFP 85B; Kirill Kudryavtsev/AFP 56B; Kyodo News 70B; Mark Leech/Offside 24-25, 111T; Christian Liewig/TempSport/Sygma/Corbis 109T; Joel Mabanglo/AFP 86B; John MacDougall/AFP 100; Ronald Martinez 96-97; Julien Mattia/NurPhoto 42-43; Michael Mayhew/Sportsphoto/Allstar 44-45; Maddie Meyer/FIFA 23B; Robert Michael/AFP 72; Pablo Morano/BSR Agency 55, 56-57; Kazuhiro Nogi/AFP 25B; Popperfoto 18B, 35B, 44B, 50B, 77, 92, 93, 107B; Steve Powell /Allsport 49R; Gary M. Prior 64-65; Mark Ralston/AFP 42B, 43T; Eric Renard / Onze / Icon Sport 20-21, 20B; Andreas Rentz/Bongarts 45B; Rolls Press/Popperfoto 17T; Martin Rose 37R; Alessandro Sabattini 35, 46B; Roberto Schmidt/AFP 46-47, 95T; Javier Soriano/AFP 41; Simon Stacpoole/Offside 59, 59T; Andrew Surma/NurPhoto 85TL; Team 2 Sportphoto/ullstein bild 107T; Bob Thomas Sports Photography 9T, 51T, 61, 82, 88; John Todd/ISI Photos 94-95; Pedro Ugarte/AFP 40; Michael Urban/AFP 28-29; VI Images 102; Antonio Villalba/Real Madrid 13T

Shutterstock: Nic Bothma/EPA 69; Helmut Fohringer/EPA 68. Images repeated throughout the book: AlfaSmart, dimensi_design, Fourleaflover, momoforsale, Pattern_Repeat, Prachova Nataliia, top dog, Polina Tomtosova

Every effort has been made to acknowledge correctly and contact the source and/or copyright holder of each picture any unintentional errors or omissions will be corrected in future editions of this book.

WELBECK
CHILDREN'S BOOKS

SOCCER'S G.O.A.T. MOMENTS

STUNNING HIGHLIGHTS FROM **WORLD CUP** HISTORY!

CONTENTS

THE GREATEST GOALS

THE GREATEST LEGENDS

THE GREATEST GAMES

THE GREATEST RECORDS

THE GREATLY BIZARRE

THE GREATEST GOALS

From super solo dribbles to incredible volleys, and long-range stunners to well-worked team moves, it's a special moment when fans witness an awesome goal at a World Cup tournament. Hitting the net in the world's biggest competition is never easy, but when a team or player does it with incredible finesse or a fierce strike, it becomes part of soccer history! It's time to feast on our selection of the Greatest Of All Time goals from the World Cup.

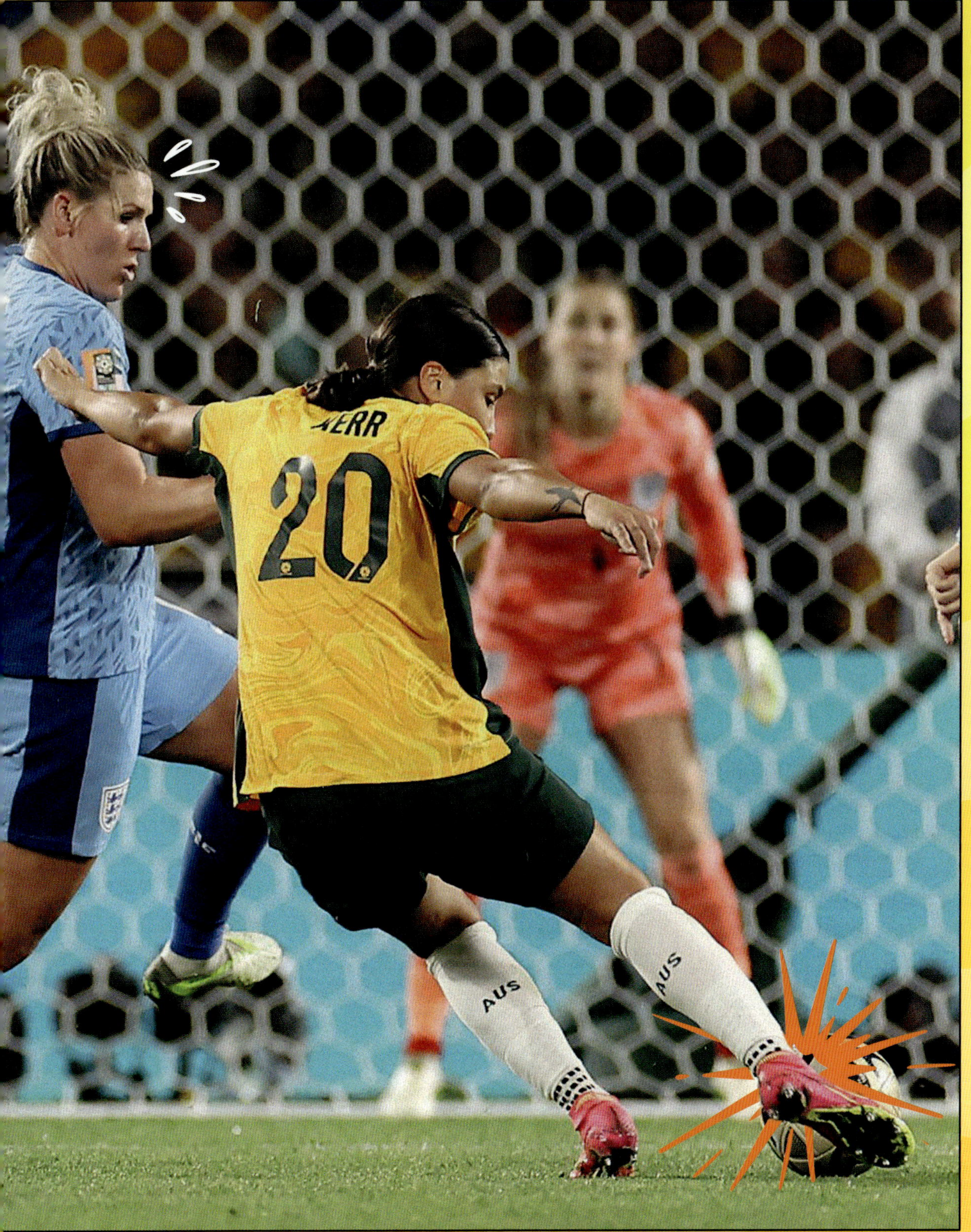
20
AUS
AUS

GOAL OF THE CENTURY!

1986 WORLD CUP QF **ARG** VS. ENG

On a scorching day in Mexico City, Diego Maradona lit up the 1986 World Cup with his red-hot second goal against England. That year the Argentina captain was the best player on the planet.

In the 55th minute Maradona collected a pass from Héctor Enrique inside his own half. With skill and quick thinking, he spun to skip away from England players Peter Beardsley and Peter Reid. Maradona then raced over the halfway line, keeping the ball glued to his left foot; he avoided Terry Butcher's fierce tackle, then danced past the final defender to reach the penalty box.

Goalkeeper Peter Shilton moved forward and dived low, but the Argentina ace jinked to the side of Shilton and as the chasing Butcher attempted another tackle, Maradona expertly fired the ball into the net. The crowd of more than 100,000 had witnessed a superstar strike with 11 perfect touches—it was a moment of magic!

DID YOU KNOW?

Maradona was 66 yards from goal when he received the ball to start his run. It took him just 11 seconds to find the net!

HAND OF GOD

Maradona showed his brilliance in scoring such a breathtaking individual goal in the quarter-final. Only a few minutes before it, though, he had opened the scoring with a sneaky handball, which became known as the "Hand of God" goal. Maradona was capable of anything on a World Cup field!

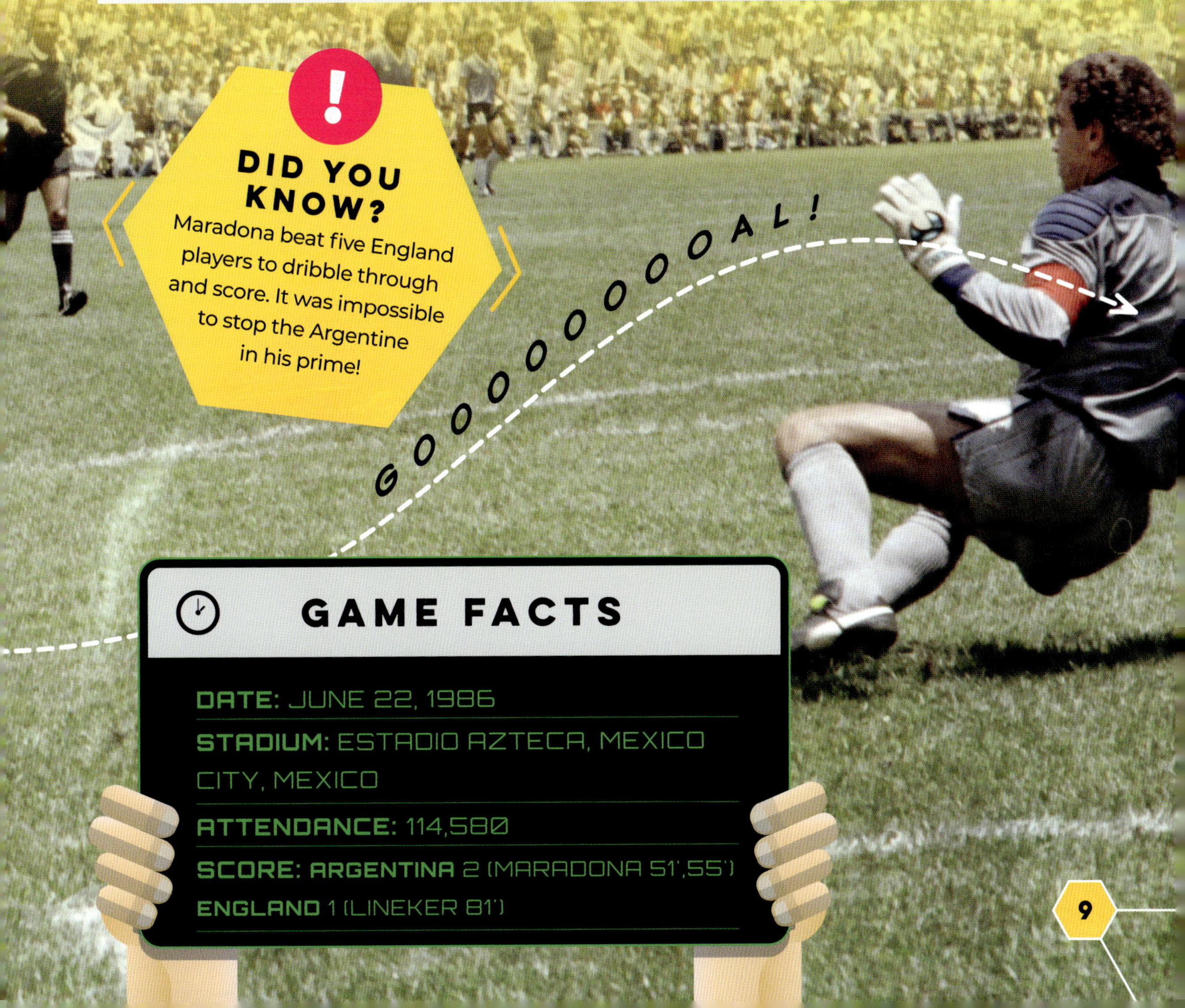

DID YOU KNOW?

Maradona beat five England players to dribble through and score. It was impossible to stop the Argentine in his prime!

GOOOOOOOOAL!

GAME FACTS

DATE: JUNE 22, 1986

STADIUM: ESTADIO AZTECA, MEXICO CITY, MEXICO

ATTENDANCE: 114,580

SCORE: ARGENTINA 2 (MARADONA 51',55')

ENGLAND 1 (LINEKER 81')

WONDER LOB

2015 WOMEN'S WORLD CUP FINAL **USA** VS. JAP

Carli Lloyd netted an outstanding long-range strike at the 2015 Women's World Cup. It was an outstanding long-range strike that capped an unbelievable hat-trick for the American superstar.

Lloyd had already shocked reigning world champions Japan with two goals inside the game's first five minutes (see pages 66-67). Her hat-trick came in the 16th minute. The attacking midfielder scooped up a loose pass inside Japan's half, knocked the ball past Japan's Rumi Utsugi, and struck a looping shot from the halfway line that dipped over goalkeeper Ayumi Kaihori.

Kaihori only managed to get her fingertips to the shot as the ball sailed over the line. The eye-catching goal put USA 4-0 ahead and en route to another World Cup win. A great moment from a great player!

BEST BALLER

The long-ranger was voted Goal Of The Tournament ahead of 11 other nominations and helped Lloyd pick up the World Cup's Golden Ball as the competition's best player. Scoring from so far out is always memorable, but to do it with the world watching and as team captain is super special.

DID YOU KNOW?

Carli Lloyd's hat-trick goal was nominated for the 2015 FIFA Puskás Award as one of the year's top strikes.

GAME FACTS

DATE: JULY 5, 2015

STADIUM: BC PLACE STADIUM, CANADA

ATTENDANCE: 53,341

SCORE: **USA** 5 (LLOYD 3', 5', 16', HOLIDAY 14', HEATH 54') **JAPAN** 2 (OGIMI 27', JOHNSTON OG 52')

VICTORY VOLLEY

2014 WORLD CUP R016 **COL** VS. URU

Colombia's James Rodríguez ended the 2014 World Cup as one of the hottest players on the planet. He netted six goals in the competition, including a beauty in the Round of 16.

Before Colombia's knockout contest against their South American rivals Uruguay, the midfielder had already scored in each group game and caught the eye of World Cup fans around the world. In this match he rubber-stamped his superstar status with a wonder strike in the first half.

In the 28th minute, he chested a headed pass outside the box before spinning round to curl a vicious volley past the Uruguay goalkeeper. Rodríguez demonstrated perfect technique to crack in this long-ranger, eclipsing his clever solo finish against Japan in his previous game. His eye-catching performances at the tournament earned him a transfer deal to Spanish giants Real Madrid after the summer.

GAME FACTS

DATE: JUNE 28, 2014

STADIUM: ESTÁDIO MÁRIO FILHO (MARACANÃ), RIO DE JANEIRO, BRAZIL

ATTENDANCE: 73,804

SCORE: **COLOMBIA** 2 (RODRÍGUEZ 28', 50')
URUGUAY 0

ROCKING RODRÍGUEZ

His return of six goals in five games saw Rodríguez earn the 2014 World Cup Golden Boot. He scored one more than Germany's Thomas Müller. It was the first time a Colombian player had received the Golden Boot, and it gave the nation their best-ever run in a World Cup tournament.

DID YOU KNOW?

In 2019, Rodríguez made his acting debut, playing a minor role in a Colombian television series called "The Goddesses of the Ring."

KERR-BOOM!

2023 WOMEN'S WORLD CUP SEMI-FINAL AUS VS. ENG

Jointly held in Australia and New Zealand, the 2023 Women's World Cup provided Australia captain Sam Kerr a fitting stage to showcase her talent with a stunning goal against England in the semi final!

Kerr was recovering from injury and had only made two appearances as a sub before starting in this game. With her team trailing 1-0 in the second half, she dribbled forward from the halfway line and saw her opportunity as the England defense struggled to close her down, and cracked a shot from outside the penalty box.

The ball rose and looped over the goalkeeper and dropped deliciously into the net. Stadium Australia erupted as fans celebrated the shooting brilliance of their superstar forward.

FANTASTIC FOUR

The Australia striker played at the 2011 and 2015 World Cups but did not score. In 2019, Kerr netted in Australia's first game against Italy and then grabbed four in the final group match against Jamaica. Only two other players have scored three or more goals in a single Women's World Cup match: Michelle Akers in 1991 and Alex Morgan in 2019, both for USA.

DID YOU KNOW?

Sam Kerr played her first senior game for Australia when she was only 15.

GAME FACTS

DATE: AUGUST 16, 2023

STADIUM: STADIUM AUSTRALIA, SYDNEY

ATTENDANCE: 75,784

SCORE: AUSTRALIA 1 (KERR 63'

ENGLAND 3 (TOONE 36', HEMP 71', RUSSO 86')

BRAZIL'S BEAUTY

1970 WORLD CUP FINAL **BRA** VS. ITA

Carlos Alberto only played in a single World Cup tournament in 1970, but he left his mark by captaining Brazil to the trophy and scoring one of the competition's finest goals.

The powerful right-back was intelligent and skillful, blessed with the athleticism and leadership to guide his team of worldbeaters. In the final against Italy, it was late on in the second half that he received the ball on the right wing and struck a thunderous first-time shot that flew past goalkeeper Enrico Albertosi.

Carlos Alberto's stunning goal had in fact been a team effort. Prior to the strike, midfielder Clodoaldo had gone past four Italians and passed the ball to Rivellino on the left. Rivellino had then knocked it forward to Jairzinho, who passed inside to Pelé. Pelé held it up for a second as Carlos Alberto powered down the right and timed to perfection his low drive to the far post.

DID YOU KNOW?

Carlos Alberto was just 25 years old when he captained Brazil to World Cup success.

STAR TEAM

The Brazil team of the 1970 World Cup is often said to be one of the best ever to grace the competition. Aside from the brilliant Carlos Alberto, it also featured world-class icons such as Pelé, Jairzinho, Tostão, and Gérson.

GAME FACTS

DATE: JUNE 21, 1970

STADIUM: SESTADIO AZTECA, MEXICO CITY, MEXICO

ATTENDANCE: 107,412

SCORE: **BRAZIL** 4 (PELÉ 18', GÉRSON 66', JAIRZINHO 71', CARLOS ALBERTO 86')
ITALY 1' (BONINSEGNA) 37')

DENNIS THE DIVINE

1998 WORLD CUP QUARTER-FINAL **NED** VS. ARG

Dennis Bergkamp scored and assisted memorable goals throughout his glorious career. For the Netherlands the creative forward crafted a fabulous finish to beat Argentina and reach the 1998 World Cup semi-final.

With the teams tied at 1–1 and extra-time on the cards, the Netherland's defender Frank de Boer played a long diagonal pass, which Bergkamp tracked like a hawk. He cushioned the ball perfectly with his right foot inside the penalty box. He took a deft second touch to knock the ball through the legs of defender Roberto Ayala to put himself in front of goal.

Bergkamp capped off the move by dinking the ball with the outside of his right foot to curl the shot beyond goalkeeper Carlos Roa. The striker needed just three quick-fire touches to bury the ball in the net and score among the most technically perfect World Cup goals, putting his nation into the last four.

SEMIFINAL SHOOTOUT

Bergkamp scored late on to beat Argentina in the quarterfinal and Patrick Kluivert netted in the 87th minute to level the semifinal match against Brazil at 1-1. The game eventually went to a penalty shootout, which Brazil won, ending the Netherland's dream of bagging their first World Cup trophy.

GAME FACTS

DATE: JULY 4, 1998

STADIUM: STADE VÉLODROME, MARSEILLE, FRANCE

ATTENDANCE: 55,000

SCORE: **NETHERLANDS** 2 (KLUIVERT 12', BERGKAMP 90') **ARGENTINA** 1 (LÓPEZ 17')

DID YOU KNOW?

Bergkamp's goal was his 36th for the Netherlands, making him their record scorer at that time.

AL-OWAIRAN ALL THE WAY

1994 WORLD CUP GROUP STAGE **KSA** VS. BEL

Saudi Arabia made their first appearance in the World Cup finals in 1994, and made a mark when striker Saeed Al-Owairan dazzled with a brilliant solo effort against Belgium.

Up to this point, Saudi Arabia had recorded one win and one defeat in the group phase. Facing Belgium in the final group game, an inspired Al-Owairan stepped up to score in the fifth minute. Picking up the ball deep inside his own half, he dribbled forward and jinked past two Belgium players and surged forward.

Defenders Rudi Smidts and Philippe Albert both attempted tackles, but once again Al-Owairan evaded them with his clever footwork, and once in the penalty box he lifted the ball over goalkeeper Michel Preud'homme. It was truly extraordinary to witness a player from the underdog side tear through the center of the field and score such an audacious goal.

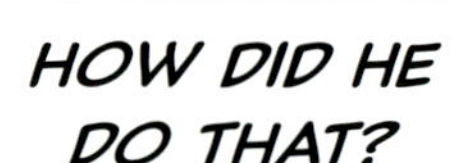

SHOOTING STAR

The goal made Al-Owairan one of the surprise stars of the World Cup. Up until that moment, he had been unknown to the rest of the world, having spent his whole career playing in the Saudi Arabian league. Al-Owairan helped his country reach the knockout stage—a super feat for a country on its debut appearance.

GAME FACTS

DATE: JUNE 29, 1994

STADIUM: RFK STADIUM, WASHINGTON, USA

ATTENDANCE: 52,959

SCORE: BELGIUM 0

SAUDI ARABIA 1 (AL-OWAIRAN 5')

DID YOU KNOW?

Al-Owairan ran 75 yards with the ball – more than two-thirds of the pitch – to score this wonder goal.

THE RISING CURLER

2015 WOMEN'S WORLD CUP R016 JAP VS. NED

Japan showed their world-class quality with one of the best team goals ever seen at the tournament. It was finished by Mizuho Sakaguchi and stunned everyone inside the stadium.

The sweeping move started with midfielder Sakaguchi winning the ball from Sherida Spitse close to the touchline. Nahomi Kawasumi knocked the ball forward to Mana Iwabuchi, who ran at the box and picked out Yuki Ogimi, while the Netherlands defense tracked back to protect their goal. Ogimi spun and took a split second to assess her next move.

She brilliantly backheeled to the overlapping Aya Miyama, who rolled the ball back toward Iwabuchi. Iwabuchi cleverly stepped over the pass, leaving Sakaguchi to curve a first-time left-foot shot through the watching defense and past goalkeeper Loes Geurts. The goal won the game 2-1 for Japan!

DID YOU KNOW?
The 2015 Women's World Cup games were all played on artificial surfaces.

GAME FACTS

DATE: JUNE 23, 2015

STADIUM: BC PLACE, VANCOUVER, CANADA

ATTENDANCE: 28,717

SCORE: **JAPAN** 2 (ARIYOSHI 10', SAKAGUCHI 78')
NETHERLANDS 1 (VAN DE VEN 90'+2)

TIGHT GAMES

Japan's six games leading up to the World Cup final were each won by a single goal margin. In the group they beat Switzerland 1-0, Cameroon 2-1, and Ecuador 1-0. The Netherlands was defeated 2-1, then Australia 1-0 in the quarter-final and England 2-1 in the semi-final. Japan lost 5–2 to USA in the final.

OUT ON HIS OWEN!

1998 WORLD CUP R016 **ENG** VS. ARG

Michael Owen was just 18 when he starred for England in 1998. His solo goal in the knockout game against rivals Argentina made the soccer world aware of his pace and composure in front of goal.

The striker had scored once in the group stage, but his next goal in a dramatic round of 16 tie against the South Americans was special. He cushioned David Beckham's pass in the center circle and burst forward, shrugging past José Chamot. He then used his lightning pace and quick feet to jink past defender Roberto Ayala, leaving only the goalkeeper to beat.

At a slight angle, Owen unleashed a right-foot shot that was beyond the reach of keeper Carlos Roa. In just a few seconds the teen star had created a goal from nothing and put England 2-1 ahead, though Argentina did equalize later on. England lost In the eventual penalty shootout, but Owen had left his mark on the competition.

DID YOU KNOW?

Jude Bellingham is the only other player to score for England at a men's World Cup tournament as a teenager.

*Argentina won 4-3 on penalties

GAME FACTS

DATE: JUNE 30, 1998

STADIUM: STADE GEOFFROY-GUICHARD, SAINT-ÉTIENNE

ATTENDANCE: 52,959

SCORE*: **ARGENTINA** 2 (BATISTUTA 5' (P) ZANETTI 45'+1)
ENGLAND 2 (SHEARER 9' OWEN 16')

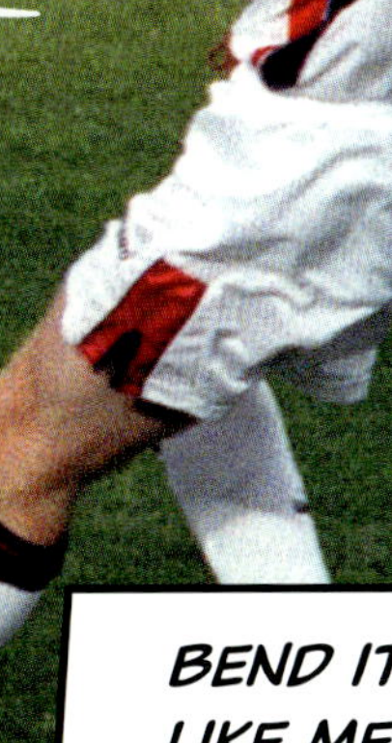

BITTER RIVALRY

England and Argentina have played each other at five World Cups. England won in 1962 and 1966, before Diego Maradona led Argentina to victory in 1986 (see pages 8-9). After the dramatic game in 1998, England got revenge in 2002 with a 1-0 group stage win thanks to David Beckham's penalty.

CAICEDO'S CLASS

2023 WOMEN'S WORLD CUP GROUP STAGE **COL** VS. GER

In the ninth edition of the Women's World Cup, Colombia's Linda Caicedo shocked double world champions Germany with a super strike in the group stage. The teen was the breakout star of the tournament.

In the 52nd minute, a shot from Manuela Vanegas dropped to Caicedo on the left side of Germany's box. She took a touch and kept the ball under close control as Sara Däbritz and Svenja Huth closed in. Caicedo waited for Huth to make a move before swiftly shifting the ball from left to right with some deft footwork.

Having created a sliver of space, Caicedo only had a fraction of a second to take a shot. Without even looking up, she swung her right foot and delicately curled the ball beyond goalkeeper Merle Frohms. The moment of magic from the teenage striker caught the Germans—and her own teammates—by surprise, and the rest is history.

YOUNG SPARK

Caicedo's extraordinary talent was evident at junior level. In 2022, she scored twice at the Under-20 Women's World Cup and later in the year she netted four times to help take Colombia to the final of the Under-17 women's tournament. Starring on the global stage comes naturally to her!

DID YOU KNOW?

Caicedo's goal was voted the best of the 2023 Women's World Cup, ahead of Marta Cox's stunning free-kick for Panama against France.

GAME FACTS

DATE: JULY 30, 2023

STADIUM: SYDNEY FOOTBALL STADIUM, SYDNEY, AUSTRALIA

ATTENDANCE: 40,499

SCORE: GERMANY 1 (POPP 89' (P))

COLOMBIA 2 (CAICEDO 52', VANEGAS 90'+7)

POETRY ON THE PITCH

2006 WORLD CUP GROUP STAGE **ARG** VS. SCG

Often considered one of the best team goals at a men's World Cup, the move was completed by defensive midfielder Esteban Cambiasso following a long series of passes as Argentina beat Serbia and Montenegro 6-0.

With the score at 1-0, Maxi Rodríguez won the ball in his own half and knocked it to Gabriel Heinze, who started the move with a pass to Javier Mascherano. Juan Riquelme and Juan Pablo Sorin took touches as the ball was sprayed around, moving from the left, to the center, and then back to the left. The patient and precise buildup continued.

A one-two between Riquelme and Javier Saviola in the final third allowed the ball to reach Cambiasso on the edge of the box. Cambiasso played a first-time pass to Hernán Crespo, who back-heeled the ball into the path Cambiasso had carved to hit a rising left-foot shot past goalkeeper Dragoslav Jevrić. With 24 passes between nine players, it was an epic team goal!

RODRÍGUEZ ROCKET

At the same tournament, Argentina scored another beautiful goal in the round of 16 tie against Mexico. The goal came in extra-time, finished by Maxi Rodríguez, who chested a long diagonal pass by Juan Pablo Sorin and struck a left-foot rocket volley that dipped over the keeper. It was Argentina's second in the team's 2-1 win.

OH BOY!
DID YOU KNOW?
Cambiasso didn't even start this game! He was a 17th-minute replacement for the injured Lucho González.
GAME FACTS
DATE: JUNE 16, 2006
STADIUM: STADION GELSENKIRCHEN, GERMANY
ATTENDANCE: 52,000
SCORE: ARGENTINA 6 (RODRÍGUEZ 6', 41' CAMBIASSO 31', CRESPO 78', TEVEZ 84', MESSI 88')
SERBIA & MONTENEGRO 0

THE *GREATEST* LEGENDS

Even though a World Cup is won by the best team, most of these teams have usually been blessed with a special player, whose brilliance plays a part in taking the team all the way to the final. These legendary figures may have wonderful skills or an ability to score from all sorts of chances, or have excellent leadership on the field. Often, they bring all of these things... and much more!

LIONEL MESSI

ARGENTINA

Lionel Messi has played at five World Cup finals and made 26 competition appearances. In the 21st century, no other player can match the magical Messi!

Messi's World Cup journey started in 2006 when he was just 18. In his first appearance at the finals, against Serbia and Montenegro, the left-footed genius scored and assisted to announce himself on the world stage. By the 2014 tournament he was Argentina captain, and his four goals helped take his team to the final, where they lost to Germany in extra-time. Four years later Messi and Argentina only reached the round of 16, but in 2022 he enjoyed his finest moment on the world stage.

MESSI'S TALLY

2006: 3 games / 1 goal

2010: 5 games / 0 goals

2014: 7 games / 4 goals

2018: 4 games / 1 goal

2022: 7 games / 7 goals

Messi celebrates Argentina's sixth goal vs. Serbia at the 2006 World Cup!

Messi has set a number of World Cup records. He has played 2,314 minutes across the five tournaments, captained his country in 19 matches, and been Player of the Match 11 times. No other Argentinian has scored as many World Cup goals (13). Messi is also the only player to have made an assist at five men's finals.

MMMWAH!

WORLD STAR MESSI

Aged 35, Messi guided Argentina to the final of the 2022 World Cup with two group stage wins and knockout victories over Australia, the Netherlands, and Croatia. In the final, he netted twice against France and won a crucial shoot-out to finally get his hands on the trophy! Messi won the Golden Ball as the best player—a prize he also took at the 2014 World Cup—and was the second-highest scorer with seven goals.

Messi kisses the World Cup trophy after Argentina's triumph in 2022!

DID YOU KNOW?

Messi is the only player to score at the World Cup in his teens, 20s, and 30s.

PELÉ

BRAZIL

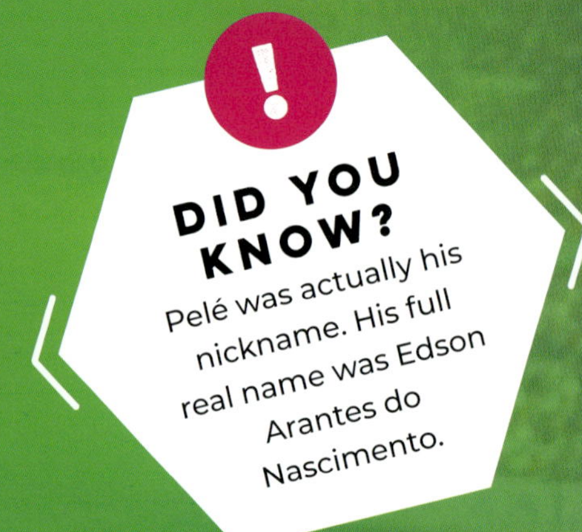

The only player to lift the World Cup trophy three times, Pelé scored in his first final in 1958 when he was just 17. His records and achievements at the tournament may never be matched.

Picked for the 1958 tournament, the teenager didn't let his nation down. Pelé scored six goals, including two in the final, helping Brazil to their first title. He became the youngest to score at a men's World Cup and also the youngest to net in a final. At the 1962 edition he played only twice because of injury, but he still picked up his second winner's medal.

In 1966 Pelé played twice and scored one goal as Brazil failed to make the knockout stage, but in 1970, he was at his best again. In the six games, the 29-year-old found the net four times, which included his headed goal in the final. Pelé's performances in the 1970 edition solidified his legacy as one of the greatest World Cup players of all time.

PELÉ BY NUMBERS

4 World Cup tournaments

3 World Cup winner's medals

14 World Cup games

12 World Cup goals

8 World Cup assists

Pelé lifts the Jules Rimet Trophy after Brazil's victory at the 1958 World Cup.

Pelé is hoisted up by his teammates after Brazil's 4-1 victory over Italy in the 1970 World Cup final.

ACING THE ASSISTS

With six to his name at the 1970 edition, Pelé tops the list for most assists at a single World Cup tournamant. The figure is one more than those recorded by Robert Gadocha (Poland) in 1974, Diego Maradona (Argentina) in 1986, Pierre Littbarski, in 1990 (Germany), and Thomas Hassler in 1994 (Germany).

ALEX MORGAN

USA

She's played in three World Cup finals, won the trophy twice, set goal-scoring records, and has made lots of memories along the way. Alex Morgan is a true great of the World Cup!

Morgan made her World Cup debut against North Korea in 2011. In the semifinal tie, she came off the bench to score against France, and repeated the feat against Japan in the final (though USA eventually lost on penalties). She returned in the 2015 edition, but this time helped her side win the trophy, beating Japan in the final.

The forward was in peak form four years later, guiding the USA to back-to-back World Cup wins. She started with five goals against Thailand, equaling Michelle Akers' 1991 record in a single game, then netting in the semi-final to beat England before scoring in another final victory against the Netherlands. Morgan is among the great names of the USA's second golden era.

Morgan kisses the trophy after USA wins the World Cup in 2019.

MORGAN'S TALLY

2011: 5 games / 2 goals

2015: 7 games / 1 goal

2019: 6 games / 6 goals

2023: 4 games / 0 goals

Morgan's 14-year international career saw her net 123 goals in 224 matches.

LUCKY FOR ALEX

Morgan wore shirt number 13 throughout her World Cup career and apart from losing in her first World Cup final, it was not an unlucky number. The Thailand goalkeeper was definitely sick of the sight of Morgan after she smashed five goals past her in 2019... in a 13-0 victory!

DID YOU KNOW?

Morgan also won the 2008 women's Under-20 World Cup, scoring in the final against North Korea.

KYLIAN MBAPPÉ

FRANCE

Kylian Mbappé is a World Cup legend! In 2018, the teen forward netted four times as France lifted the trophy. In doing so, he equaled Pele's record of scoring the most goals in a World Cup tournament as a teenager.

Four years later Mbappé was at it again. The 2022 edition in Qatar saw the forward score three goals during the group stage and twice against Poland in the round of 16. Mbappé was tied with Lionel Messi on five before the final with Argentina (see pages 56-57). His stunning hat-trick gave him the Golden Boot with eight goals.

Only four other players have scored in two men's World Cup final matches. Mbappé was the Silver Ball winner in 2022 to add to his Young Player prize from 2018. Will Mbappé add to his tally in 2026? Most likely.

DID YOU KNOW?

Mbappe is friends with NBA superstar LeBron James and has been pictured with LeBron multiple times.

MBAPPÉ BY NUMBERS

- **2** World Cup tournaments
- **1** World Cup winner's medal
- **14** World Cup games
- **12** World Cup goals
- **3** World Cup assists
- **3** World Cup awards

Mbappé performs his iconic goal celebration after scoring in the final of the 2022 World Cup.

Mbappé on his way to his hat-trick against Argentina in the 2022 World Cup final!

HAT-TRICK HERO

Mbappé's hat-trick against Argentina in 2022 made him just the second player to achieve this feat in a men's World Cup final. The first was Geoff Hurst in the 1966 final when England beat Germany 4–2 (see pages 74-75). Mbappé's total of four World Cup final goals is also a record in the men's tournament.

DID YOU KNOW?

Mbappé's volley in the 2022 World Cup final was clocked at 77 mph (124 km/h)—the speediest scoring shot at the finals!

MIROSLAV KLOSE

GERMANY

The German forward holds the record for most goals scored at the men's World Cup. His tally of 16 strikes puts him one ahead of Brazil's Ronaldo. Klose's 16th goal came during the 7-1 demolition of Brazil in 2014.

Klose started his World Cup career in 2002 with a hat-trick of headers in an 8-0 win against Saudi Arabia. He bagged five in the tournament as Germany were runners-up in the final to Brazil. In 2006, the striker collected another five goals to win the Golden Shoe (Golden Boot).

His third tournament in 2010 was again full of goals as he scored against Australia, England, and a double to help beat Argentina. Still chasing glory at the age of 36 in 2014, Klose finally became a world champion as Germany saw off Argentina 1-0 in the final, and he wrote himself into the book of the World Cup's greatest-ever performers.

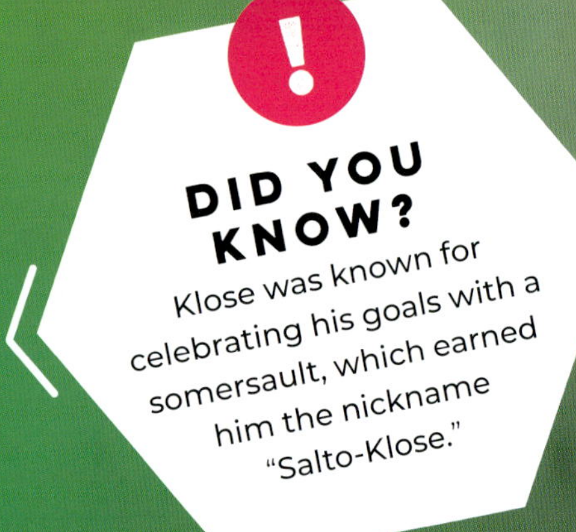

KLOSE'S TALLY

2002: 7 games / 5 goals

2006: 7 games / 5 goals

2010: 5 games / 4 goals

2014: 5 games / 2 goals

Klose scored a hat-trick on his World Cup debut against Saudi Arabia in 2002.

MEDAL MAN

Not only does Klose hold the record for the most goals scored in men's World Cup history, but he is the only player to pick up a medal at four tournaments. With gold in 2014, silver in 2002, and bronze at the 2010 and 2006 finals, his cabinet is packed!

Klose celebrates after scoring against Ghana in the group stage game in the 2014 World Cup.

!

DID YOU KNOW?

Klose's 17 World Cup match wins across four editions is the most of any male player.

MARTA

BRAZIL

Skillful, fast, and spectacular, Marta is a World Cup icon. Playing in six finals, the number 10 netted a record 17 goals and is widely considered one of the greatest female soccer players of all time.

In 2007, during the semifinal match against the mighty USA, Marta showed her magnificence. She scored in the first half to put Brazil 2-0 ahead and then delivered an amazing goal at 79 minutes to cap a 4-0 win. Marta flicked the ball past her marker, then raced into the box to beat a defender and fire a low shot into the net.

Marta converts a spot kick against Italy at the 2019 World Cup to become the all-time top scorer at men's or women's finals.

MARTA BY NUMBERS

- **6** World Cup tournaments
- **0** World Cup winner's medals
- **23** World Cup games
- **17** World Cup goals
- **5** World Cup assists
- **3** World Cup awards

An in-form Marta celebrates after scoring her second goal against the USA at the 2007 edition.

Marta's historic 17th World Cup goal was a penalty against Italy at the 2019 event in France. In that competition the Brazil captain also became the first to score at five Women's World Cups. Marta was also honored as World Player of the Year six times during her career!

MARTA'S MOMENT

The 2007 World Cup final didn't see Marta lift the trophy, but her runners-up medal was the first of three she took at the tournament. At age 21, she finished as Golden Boot winner with seven goals and was voted best player of the finals and awarded the Golden Ball.

DID YOU KNOW?

Besides her feats in the World Cup, Marta was the first player to score in five consecutive Olympic Games, between 2004 and 2020*!

*Games took place in 2021 because of the COVID pandemic.

ZINEDINE ZIDANE

FRANCE

I'M A POET WITH THE BALL.

Legendary playmaker Zinedine Zidane featured in three World Cup competitions and was a key figure in each. His goals and creative genius helped France win the trophy for the first time in 1998.

With France hosting the 1998 competition, there was pressure on Zidane to perform as the team's talisman. He sparkled in their first group stage win, but was red carded in the next match. He returned in the knockout stage to help beat Italy and the Netherlands to reach the final in Paris, where "Zizou" scored twice as France became champions.

Zidane showcases his ball skills against Denmark at the 2002 World Cup.

ZIDANE BY NUMBERS

3	World Cup tournaments
1	World Cup winner's medal
12	World Cup games
5	World Cup goals
5	World Cup assists
1	World Cup Golden Ball

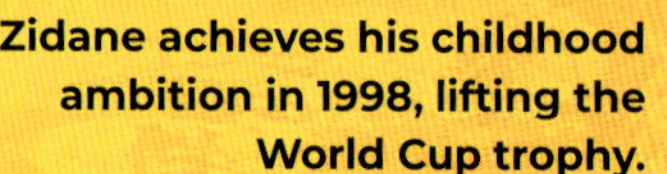

Zidane achieves his childhood ambition in 1998, lifting the World Cup trophy.

Zidane's goals in a dominant 3-0 final win over reigning champions Brazil were all headers, something the great man did not specialize in. Coming in the 27th minute and first half injury-time, he scored both from corner kicks as he powerfully directed the ball beyond goalkeeper Taffarel. It was party time in the streets of Paris!

DID YOU KNOW?

When Zidane was 14, he was inspired by watching Diego Maradona win the World Cup with Argentina in 1986.

MISSING MAN

The 2002 World Cup turned into a nightmare for both France and Zidane. Before it started, Zidane was out with an injured thigh and the team lost 1-0 and drew 0-0 in their first two games. He played in the third game but wasn't fully fit and France finished bottom. His next World Cup in 2006 would be more eventful, though for the wrong reason (see page 100).

RONALDO

BRAZIL

DID YOU KNOW?
Eleven 17-year-olds have been to a men's World Cup, but only Pelé (1958) and Ronaldo (1994) won it at that young age.

With 15 goals and two winner's medals across four editions, Ronaldo Nazario's name shines in the annals of World Cup history.

Ronaldo was a surprise selection for the 1994 World Cup when he was just 17. Although he didn't play, he received a winner's medal as a squad member. At the 1998 World Cup, he was Brazil's star player, scoring four goals in seven games and taking Brazil to the final. He was in inspired form in 2002, finishing as a World Cup champion and Golden Boot winner after netting both goals against Germany in the final.

RONALDO'S TALLY

1994: 0 games / 0 goals

1998: 7 games / 4 goals

2002: 7 games / 8 goals

2006: 5 games / 3 goals

Ronaldo is on top of the world after taking Brazil to glory at the 2002 World Cup.

Ronaldo rounds the Ghanaian keeper to score his 15th World Cup goal at the 2006 edition.

FINAL FLOURISH

Ronaldo's 15th and final World Cup goal was scored in typical style. He was one-on-one with Ghana goalkeeper Richard Kingson (left), then sent him the wrong way as he rounded through to coolly hit the net. It made him the all-time top scorer until Miroslav Klose reached 16 in 2014 (see pages 40–41).

DID YOU KNOW?

Ronaldo played for Brazil in 98 matches, scoring 62 goals, and is the third-highest goal scorer for his national team.

The 2006 World Cup saw the striker net his 15th competition goal against Ghana, beating the previous record of 14 by Germany's Gerd Müller. Brazil fell at the quarterfinals and Ronaldo's World Cup story came to an end, but his achievements and impact will always be a celebrated part of World Cup history.

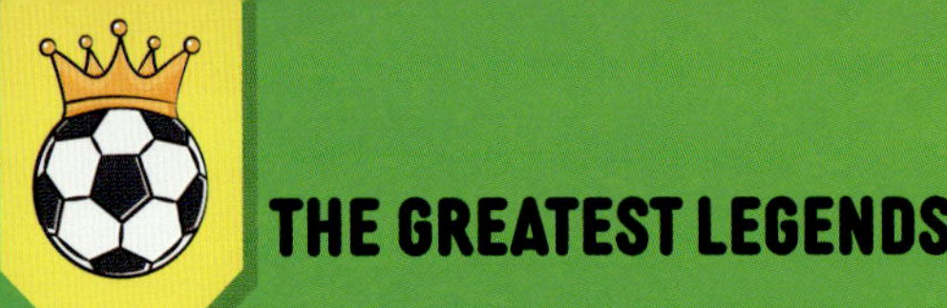

DIEGO MARADONA

ARGENTINA

Maradona's moment of superstardom as he lifts the trophy at the 1986 World Cup.

Diego Maradona's wonder performances made him a star across four World Cup competitions. He played in two finals and lifted the trophy as captain when Argentina beat Germany in 1986.

Making is World Cup debut in 1982, he netted twice against Hungary in the group stage. But, it was in 1986 that he took the finals by storm. Five goals, including his famous double to beat England, guided his country to glory. In 1990, his vision and leadership took Argentina to another final against Germany, as he narrowly missed out on consecutive winner's medals by a single goal.

MARADONA'S TALLY

1982: 5 games / 2 goals

1986: 7 games / 5 goals

1990: 7 games / 0 goals

1994: 2 games / 1 goal

Maradona coolly finishes his fine solo effort against England at the 1986 World Cup.

Maradona's final World Cup was at USA 1994. He scored once with a thunderbolt shot against Greece. However, after Argentina's second game he tested positive for a banned stimulant and was sent home. It was a chaotic end to a scintillating World Cup career.

FAMOUS PHOTO

Argentina played Belgium at the 1982 World Cup. This image shows six Belgian players trying to defend against Maradona, but it's a little misleading because Diego had actually received a short pass from a free kick and the Belgians shown had broken from their defensive wall. Still, it is a classic photo!

DID YOU KNOW?

Maradona was involved in 10 of Argentina's 14 World Cup goals in the 1986 World Cup (five goals and five assists).

DID YOU KNOW?

Maradona was so skilful and fast he was fouled a record 152 times at the World Cup. Opponents struggled to stop him!

FRANZ BECKENBAUER

GERMANY

Because of his leadership and winning mentality, German legend Franz Beckenbauer was known as "Der Kaiser," meaning the Emperor. He belongs to a rare group who have enjoyed World Cup glory as both player and coach.

On his World Cup debut in 1966, Beckenbauer played in midfield and scored twice against Switzerland, then scored again in the quarterfinals and semifinals, before the team lost to England in the final (see pages 74–75). At the 1970 edition, he struck a fine goal against England in the quarters, but the team lost to Italy at the semifinal stage. He played that game with a dislocated shoulder following a strong tackle.

The 1974 World Cup was hosted by Germany and with the home support, Beckenbauer finally landed the top international prize. Now playing as captain and a defensive sweeper, he used his expert technique to control games, beating the Netherlands 2-1 in the final and celebrated with the trophy at Munich's Olympic Stadium.

BECKENBAUER BY NUMBERS

3	World Cup tournaments
1	World Cup winner's medal
18	World Cup games
5	World Cup goals
3	World Cup All-Star Teams
1	Ballon d'Or

Beckenbauer was in top form against the Netherlands in the 1974 final.

DOUBLE DELIGHT

Beckenbauer became Germany manager in 1984 and he took the team to the 1986 World Cup final. They lost that game to Argentina, but four years later, with the two nations contesting the final again, Germany won 1-0. Beckenbauer was the second person (after Mario Zagallo of Brazil) to win the World Cup as player and then as coach.

DID YOU KNOW?

In 1974, Beckenbauer was the first captain to lift the new World Cup trophy after Brazil were gifted the original Jules Rimet trophy in 1970.

AITANA BONMATÍ

SPAIN

Spain's classy midfielder shone throughout the 2023 World Cup. Aitana Bonmatí's fine scoring and assisting skills gave her country a ruthless attacking edge.

From Bonmatí's seven games at the 2023 competition, she recorded three goals, two assists, and two player of the match awards. Against Switzerland in the round of 16, she scored twice with skillful left-foot finishes. In the final, Bonmatí bossed the midfield against England and took her team to their first World Cup trophy.

VAMMMOSSS!

BONMATÍ IN NUMBERS

- **2** World Cup tournaments
- **1** World Cup winner's medal
- **9** World Cup games
- **3** World Cup goals
- **2** World Cup assists
- **1** World Cup Golden Ball

Bonmatí controls play against England in the 2023 World Cup final.

Bonmatí also played twice at the 2019 edition, making substitute appearances as a 21-year-old – experiences that undoubtedly paved the way for future greatness. In fact, coming into the 2023 showdown, she had achieved domestic and European success with club giants Barcelona, and was considered the best female player on the planet.

AWARD WINNERS

Bonmatí scooped the Golden Ball prize in 2023 and her eye-catching Spanish teammates also picked up individual honours. Forward Jenni Hermoso was the Silver Ball winner, awarded to the second-best player, and winger Salma Paralluelo was named the Best Young Player.

DID YOU KNOW?

At the 2023 World Cup, Bonmatí completed 327 passes, had 20 shots, and created 11 scoring chances for Spain.

Bonmatí celebrates after netting against Costa Rica in the group stage of the 2023 World Cup.

DID YOU KNOW?

Bonmatí helped Spain reach the final of the Under-20 World Cup in 2018.

THE GREATEST GAMES

We've picked some of the most memorable matches in the history of the men's and women's World Cup, featuring big hitters such as Brazil, Argentina, USA, France, Germany, England, and Italy. So whether it's for a late goal, a high score, a breathtaking finish, or an impressive comeback, soccer supporters famously remember the following 10 games as among the World Cup's greatest spectacles!

FIFA WORLD CUP

ARGENTINA vs. FRANCE

3-3*

2022 WORLD CUP **FINAL**

*Argentina wins 4-2 on penalties

The 64th and decisive game at the 2022 World Cup was a cracker! With the world's two best frontmen facing off, the final delivered lots of goals and unforgettable drama all the way to the final whistle.

Argentina took control in the early stages. Lionel Messi converted from the penalty spot and 13 minutes later it was 2-0 as Ángel Di María swept home a shot inside the penalty box. The South Americans were closing in on the trophy until the magnificent Kylian Mbappé struck in the 80th and 81st minutes with a penalty and a rocket volley.

TOP TENS

Lionel Messi and Kylian Mbappé both wore the number ten shirt for their respective teams. Although rivals at the 2022 World Cup, the legendary pair were actually club teammates at the time. They both played for French team Paris Saint-Germain from 2021 to 2023.

In the first half of extra time, Messi once again put his country in front, pouncing on a rebound from keeper Lloris. But, in the dying seconds, France was awarded a penalty, which Mbappé put away to level the match and take it to a dramatic shootout. France failed to score two spot kicks, leaving Gonzalo Montiel to net and send the Argentina fans into rapture.

DID YOU KNOW?

According to FIFA estimates, a record 1.5 billion people tuned in to watch the 2022 World Cup final on screens around the world.

Argentina captain Lionel Messi raises the World Cup trophy after guiding his team to a historic win.

GAME FACTS

DATE: DECEMBER 18, 2022

STADIUM: LUSAIL STADIUM, LUSAIL, QATAR

ATTENDANCE: 88,966

SCORE: ARGENTINA 3 (MESSI 23', 108', DI MARÍA 36') **FRANCE** 3 (MBAPPÉ 80', 81', 118')

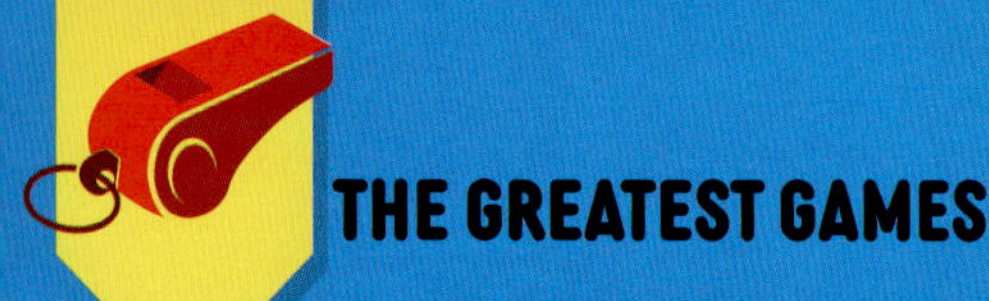

BRAZIL vs. GERMANY

Brazil hosted the 2014 World Cup and had aspirations to reach the final and lift the trophy in front of their fans. That dream turned into a nightmare when they came up against an inspired Germany in the semi-final tie!

André Schürrle celebrates scoring Germany's seventh and rounds off the goal rout against hosts Brazil.

Germany took just 11 minutes to score when an unmarked Thomas Müller volleyed from close range. Four goals came in a devastating six-minute spell as Miroslav Klose, a double from Toni Kroos, and Sami Khedira struck to make it 5-0 at half-time. The Brazil fans in the packed stadium were stunned into silence.

With Brazil in complete disarray, André Schürrle bagged twice in the second half to make it seven for Germany before Brazil pulled one back in the 90th minute. The record defeat wrecked Brazil's hopes of a sixth World Cup at the famous Maracanã Stadium. For German players and supporters it was an unforgettable night!

GAME FACTS

DATE: JULY 8, 2014

STADIUM: ESTÁDIO MINEIRÃO, BELO HORIZONTE, BRAZIL

ATTENDANCE: 58,141

SCORE: BRAZIL 1 (OSCAR 90')

GERMANY 7 (MÜLLER 11', KLOSE 23', KROOS 24', 26', KHEDIRA 29', SCHÜRRLE 69', 79')

WEAKENED BY INJURY?

In Brazil's defense, they were forced to play the match without their superstar striker Neymar. Neymar had four goals in the tournament but was sidelined with an injury he picked up in the 2-1 quarterfinal win over Colombia. Key defender Thiago Silva also missed the game because of suspension.

DID YOU KNOW?

This was the first time a team had scored seven goals in a World Cup semifinal. In doing so, Germany had also avenged the 2-0 defeat they suffered against Brazil in the 2002 World Cup final.

NORWAY vs. USA

Held in 1991, the first FIFA Women's World Cup saw the USA become champion of this groundbreaking tournament. With 63,000 fans watching the final in China, it was a significant moment in the sport, paving the way for the growth of the women's game.

The first Women's World Cup final was a dramatic clash between Norway and USA. The opening goal was a powerful header scored by USA's star striker Michelle Akers (see pages 88-89). Norway's Linda Medalen equalized nine minutes later with another excellent headed goal.

As both teams searched for a winner, it was Akers who struck again in the 78th minute. She pounced on a defensive mistake by Tina Svensson and dribbled around the Norway goalkeeper to sweep the ball home.

A STAR IS BORN

In 1991, USA was packed with stars such as Michelle Akers, Carin Jennings, and April Heinrichs. The team also featured Mia Hamm, a gifted teenage attacker. Only 19 at this World Cup, Hamm scored twice in the group stage and started in the final. Hamm would go on to become an all-time great and win the trophy again in 1999.

DID YOU KNOW?
All the games at the 1991 FIFA Women's World Cup were 80 minutes long instead of the usual 90.

Team USA are jubilant as they edge out Norway and win the first Women's World Cup trophy.

GAME FACTS

DATE: NOVEMBER 30, 1991

STADIUM: TIANHE STADIUM, GUANGZHOU, CHINA

ATTENDANCE: 63,000

SCORE: NORWAY 1 (MEDALEN 29')

USA 2 (AKERS 20', 78')

ITALY vs. GERMANY

4-3

1970 WORLD CUP **SEMIFINAL**

When these two giants of soccer locked horns in the 1970 semifinal, not only did the game feature lots of goals, but with the majority coming in extra-time, the outcome seesawed during the final stages, creating edge-of-the-seat drama!

Roberto Boninsegna scored a fine opener for Italy from the edge of the box at eight minutes. Germany couldn't hit back and Italy defended strongly. Amazingly, Karl-Heinz Schnellinger scored in the 92nd minute to force extra-time.

A thrilling half hour followed. Germany striker Gerd Müller put his team ahead, but Tarcisio Burgnich made it 2-2. Luigi Riva's goal put the score at 3-2 to Italy at the end of the first half of extra-time. Müller hit back to make it 3-3. However, it was Giovanni Rivera's strike only a minute later that put Italy into the final.

DID YOU KNOW?

The semifinal tie is often called the Game of the Century. The five goals scored in extra-time is a record at a World Cup.

Italy rejoice after scoring their fourth goal in the 111th minute, clinching victory against Germany and a place in the final.

DAY OF THE DEFENDER

Germany had an unlikely scorer to thank for taking this extraordinary game into extra-time. Karl-Heinz Schnellinger's strike in injury time was the only time he scored for his country in 47 games. In 1970, the defender was actually playing club soccer in Italy with AC Milan.

GAME FACTS

DATE: JUNE 17, 1970

STADIUM: ESTADIO AZTECA, MEXICO CITY, MEXICO

ATTENDANCE: 102,444

SCORE: ITALY 4 (BONINSEGNA 8', BURGNICH 98', RIVA 104', RIVERA 111')
GERMANY 3 (SCHNELLINGER 90'+2, MÜLLER 94', 110')

KOREA REP. vs. ITALY

2-1

2002 WORLD CUP
ROUND OF 16

Italy entered the 2002 tournament as three-time World Cup winners. Cohost South Korea had only ever played at two finals and never won. Get ready for a shock by the Taegeuk Warriors!

South Korea's Ahn Jung-hwan heads the winning goal past Italy goalkeeper Gianluigi Buffon.

GAME FACTS

DATE: JUNE 18, 2002

STADIUM: DAEJEON WORLD CUP STADIUM, REP. OF KOREA

ATTENDANCE: 38,588

SCORE: KOREA REP. 2 (KI-HYEON 88', JUNG-HWAN 117') **ITALY** 1 (VIERI 18')

HISTORY ON REPEAT

In 2002, Italy was devastated to lose to South Korea after leading until the 88th minute. Incidentally, at the 1966 World Cup, Italy was knocked out at the group stage after suffering an unexpected 1-0 loss—this time to North Korea.

Italy started this knockout game as huge favorites, but survived a big scare in the fifth minute when Ahn Jung-hwan had a penalty saved. The team then took the lead with Christian Vieri's 18th-minute header and in typical Italian style, their defense thwarted all South Korea attacks. Cheered on by the crowd, South Korea never gave up!

In the 88th minute, Seol Ki-hyeon sent the stadium wild as he lashed a left-foot shot beyond goalkeeper Gianluigi Buffon. It forced extra-time and the chance for South Korea to score a golden goal. That moment arrived with just three minutes left when Ahn Jung-hwan headed the ball home from a cross (see page 112).

DID YOU KNOW?

South Korea went on to beat Spain in the quarterfinals to become the first Asian team to reach a men's World Cup semifinal.

USA vs. JAPAN

5-2

2015 WOMEN'S WORLD CUP **FINAL**

Packed with goals, the 2015 Women's World Cup showpiece final lived up to its billing. The match was full of magical moments and memorable goals. For USA it delivered a third World Cup crown!

It was a clash of giants and a repeat of the 2011 World Cup final, which Japan had won on penalties. USA raced into a stunning four-goal lead as captain Carli Lloyd scored twice from close range in the first five minutes. Lauren Holiday made it 3-0 in the 14th minute and two minutes later, Lloyd lofted in a lob from the halfway line to complete her hat-trick and make it 4–0!

Japan finally hit back in the 27th minute as Yuki Ogimi curled the ball into the net from inside the box. An own goal by USA's Julie Johnston early in the second half gave Japan a glimmer of hope. But the hope was dashed by Tobin Heath's low strike two minutes later and the match finished 5-2. Overall, America's five-star display made them world champions once again!

All hands on the trophy as USA celebrate victory over Japan to win the 2015 World Cup!

HOPE'S GLORY

It is usually the goal scorers who bask in the glory, but it was USA's goalkeeper Hope Solo who won the plaudits at the 2015 World Cup. She won the Golden Glove as the best keeper for the second World Cup in a row, after keeping five clean sheets to reach the final. No other player has won the prize twice.

DID YOU KNOW?

Carli Lloyd's hat-trick in the first 16 minutes was the quickest in World Cup history and the only triple strike in a women's final.

GAME FACTS

DATE: JULY 5, 2015

STADIUM: BC PLACE STADIUM, CANADA

ATTENDANCE: 53,341

SCORE: USA 5 (LLOYD 3', 5', 16', HOLIDAY 14', HEATH 54') **JAPAN** 2 (OGIMI 27', JOHNSTON OG 52')

PORTUGAL vs. KOREA DPR

7-0

2010 WORLD CUP
GROUP STAGE

As the heavens opened during a World Cup game in South Africa, the goals rained down on the pitch. Portugal had drawn 0-0 with Ivory Coast in their opening Group G match, but six days later they had their shooting cleats on against North Korea!

The first half had been competitive with only a goal from Portugal's Raul Meireles separating the nations at the break. Simão made it 2-0 on 53 minutes and seven minutes later the lead was doubled to 4-0. Three strikes in the last ten minutes completed the demolition job.

Hugo Almeida of Portugal expertly beats North Korea's keeper Ri Myong-guk to score his team's third goal.

THE WAIT IS OVER

Captain Cristiano Ronaldo's goal in the 87th minute was the result of both skill and good fortune. The ball flicked up and dropped on his back, before kindly rolling off his head and dropping for a cool right-foot volley. This was a mighty moment for Ronaldo as, for him, it ended a goal drought that had stretched to 11 international games.

GAME FACTS
DATE: JUNE 21, 2010
STADIUM: CAPE TOWN STADIUM, SOUTH AFRICA
ATTENDANCE: 63,644
SCORE: PORTUGAL 7 (MEIRELES 29', SIMÃO 53', ALMEIDA 56', TIAGO 60', 89', LIÉDSON 81', RONALDO 87') NORTH KOREA 0
WHERE'S THE BALL?
DID YOU KNOW?
In a group labeled the "Group of Death," North Korea failed to pick up a single point in 2010, conceding 12 goals in three games!

FRANCE VS. ARGENTINA

2018 WORLD CUP
ROUND OF 16

This spectacular knockout clash between France and Argentina was worthy of a World Cup final match. The match was a seesawing affair packed with star players, high-quality goals, and end-to-end excitement.

PAVARD POWER!

France's Benjamin Pavard struck a breathtaking goal, which would later be awarded Goal of the Tournament. Defender Lucas Hernandez crossed the ball from deep on the left and it came through to the edge of the box, where Pavard met it with a half volley that rose and curled inside the far post.

France took an early lead with Antoine Griezmann converting the resulting penalty after Kylian Mbappé had been fouled in the box. Ángel Di María's left-foot rocket and Gabriel Mercado's flick put Argentina 2-1 ahead before defender Benjamin Pavard struck a brilliant effort (see opposite). Game on at 2-2!

An end-to-end match was eventually settled by Mbappé's masterclass. The teenager drilled a low left-foot shot to put France 3-2 up and struck again with a first-time effort with the right foot to make it 4-2. Sergio Agüero's late goal was just a consolation as the referee blew the whistle to bring an end to the thrilling game.

DID YOU KNOW?

Pavard's goal (opposite) was voted the best at the 2018 event, with Juan Quintero's (Colombia) second and Luka Modrić's strike (Croatia) coming third.

Kylian Mbappé coolly celebrates after scoring against Argentina to put France 4–2 ahead at the 2018 World Cup.

GAME FACTS

DATE: JUNE 30, 2018

STADIUM: AK BARS ARENA, KAZAN, RUSSIA

ATTENDANCE: 42,873

SCORE: **FRANCE** 4 (GRIEZMANN 13' (P), PAVARD 57', MBAPPÉ 64', 68') **ARGENTINA** 3 (DI MARÍA 41', MERCADO 48', AGÜERO 90'+3)

BRAZIL vs. USA

With Brazil stars Marta, Cristiane, and Formiga facing off against USA's heroes Carli Lloyd, Abby Wambach, and Hope Solo, this tie promised to be a tantalizing encounter, and so it proved, turning into a World Cup classic!

Brazil went 1-0 down after just 78 seconds as Daiane netted an own goal. It stayed that way until the 68th minute when USA's Rachel Buehler was sent off for fouling in the box and the ref awarded Brazil a penalty. Dramatically, Brazil's Cristiane missed the spot-kick, but the referee ordered a retake, which Marta converted.

In the final phases of extra-time, the skillful Marta struck from a tight angle, putting Brazil 2-1 up and seemingly into the semis. However, the game's final attack saw USA's Wambach power a header in, taking the match to a penalty shoot-out. Daiane's kick in the shoot-out was saved and Ali Krieger scored hers to earn USA a sensational win!

SWEET REVENGE

USA players took great joy in knocking out Brazil, even if the win was by a penalty shootout. At the previous World Cup, it was the South Americans who outclassed the Stars and Stripes, winning 4-0 to book a place in the World Cup final with Germany.

DID YOU KNOW?

USA defender Ali Krieger was hailed a hero for scoring the vital penalty in the shoot-out and earned the nickname Warrior Princess!

GAME FACTS

DATE: JULY 10, 2011

STADIUM: RUDOLF-HARBIG-STADION, DRESDEN, GERMANY

ATTENDANCE: 25,598

SCORE: BRAZIL 2 (MARTA 68', 92')

USA 2 (DAIANE 2' OG, WAMBACH 120'+2)

USA keeper Hope Solo is jubilant after making the vital save in the shoot-out.

ENGLAND vs. GERMANY

1966 WORLD CUP **FINAL**

England's greatest soccer success on the international stage came in 1966—the year England hosted the World Cup. On a Saturday afternoon in July, the team tussled with Germany in what turned out to be a thrilling final.

Germany took the lead on 12 minutes to silence the home crowd, but Geoff Hurst headed the equalizer six minutes later, re-energizing the home fans. When England midfielder Martin Peters netted from close range at 78 minutes, the Wembley crowd roared with excitement, but Germany's Wolfgang Weber struck in the final minute to take the game into extra-time.

England had some luck when Hurst got his second goal. The referee and linesman both agreed the ball had crossed the line, when it wasn't clear whether it did or not. Hurst then made sure of the victory as he raced away in the 120th minute and smashed a near-post shot past the German goalkeeper for his World Cup final hat-trick.

HAMMER TIME

English club West Ham United can claim they played a big part in helping the national team win the World Cup in 1966. Captain and defensive leader Bobby Moore (below), hat-trick hero Hurst and Peters—the scorer of England's second goal—all played for the club at the time and went on to become club legends.

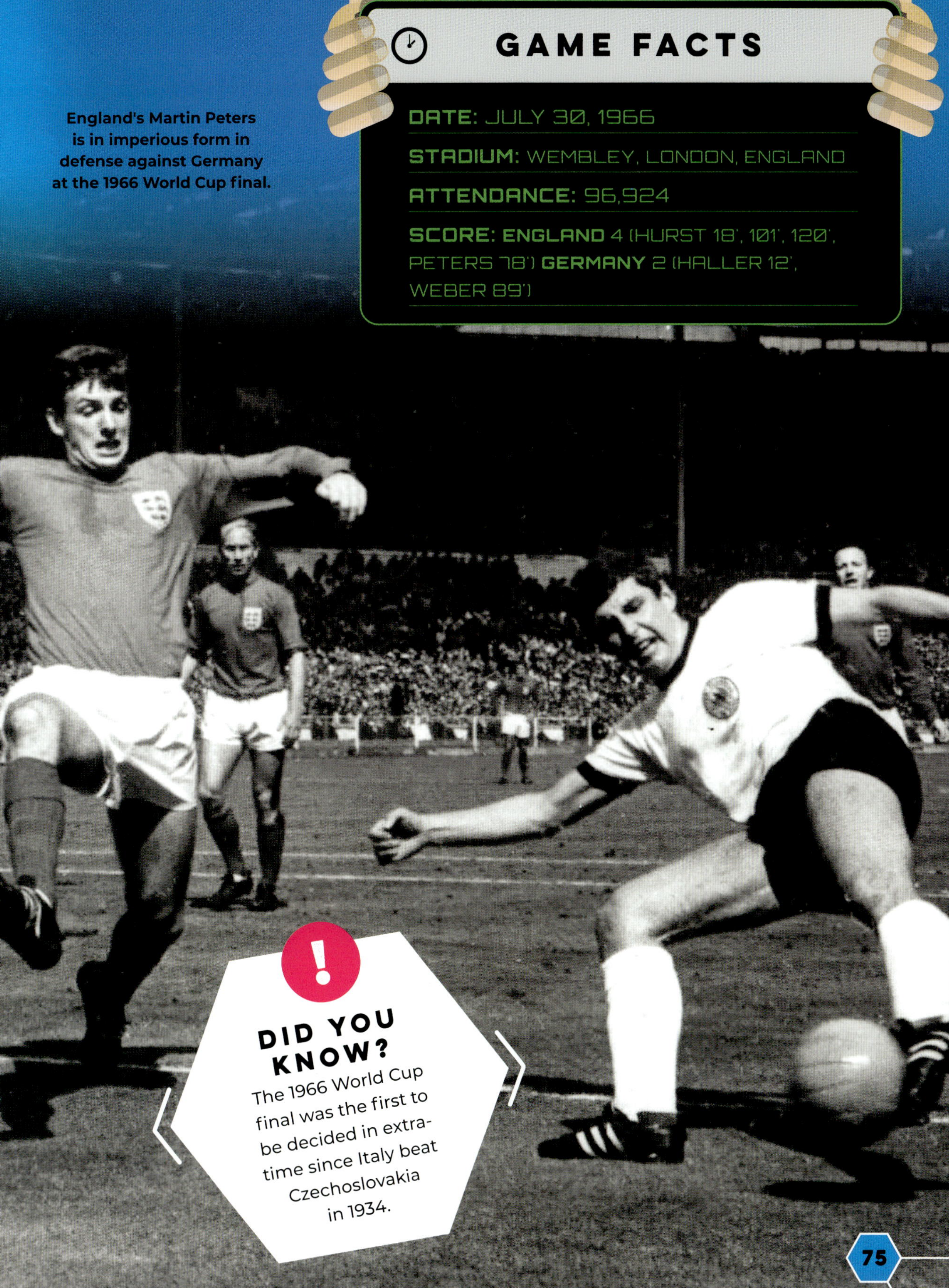

GAME FACTS

DATE: JULY 30, 1966

STADIUM: WEMBLEY, LONDON, ENGLAND

ATTENDANCE: 96,924

SCORE: **ENGLAND** 4 (HURST 18', 101', 120', PETERS 78') **GERMANY** 2 (HALLER 12', WEBER 89')

England's Martin Peters is in imperious form in defense against Germany at the 1966 World Cup final.

DID YOU KNOW?

The 1966 World Cup final was the first to be decided in extra-time since Italy beat Czechoslovakia in 1934.

THE *GREATEST* RECORDS

It's time to dive into the top stats, facts, and exciting achievements set by players and teams during the World Cup's long history. From goal-hungry strikers to fantastic finalists, shock results, great goalkeepers, and hat-trick heroes, the competition has produced many memorable records and sensational stories. Turn over to kick off your journey through the World Cup record books!

SUPER STRIKER

13 GOALS!
1958 WORLD CUP

The World Cup has seen many magnificant strikers, but none can match Just Fontaine's goal tally in 1958. The France hero netted 13 goals at that year's competition—the most in a single tournament.

Fontaine opened his account in the group stage with a hat-trick in a big 7-3 win over Paraguay, followed by a double against Yugoslavia and a goal in the final group game to help his team beat Scotland 2-1. In peak scoring form, he delivered two more strikes in the first knockout game to beat Northern Ireland in the quarterfinals.

In the semifinals, France came up against the mighty Brazil. The South Americans outclassed the French, but Fontaine still grabbed a goal in the 5-2 semifinal loss. His concluding appearance at the 1958 World Cup was for the third-place prize. Facing Germany he smashed in four goals as France celebrated a 6-3 win. Fontaine had 13 goals and, because of injury, he sadly never got to play at another World Cup.

DID YOU KNOW?

Fontaine played basketball as a child, which he says helped develop his agility to shake off defenders on the soccer field!

SIX IN A ROW

Fontaine had scored in six World Cup games in a row at the 1958 World Cup. He held that record until 1970 when Brazil's dazzling forward Jairzinho matched him. Jairzinho's goals came in games against Czechoslovakia, England, Romania, Peru, Uruguay, and Italy. Jairzinho may have scored fewer goals but his seventh strike helped Brazil win the trophy against Italy in the final.

Just Fontaine completes his hat-trick against Germany in the battle for third place at the 1958 World Cup.

MASTER BLASTER

HIGHEST-SCORING WORLD CUP MATCH!

2019 WOMEN'S WORLD CUP

At the 2019 Women's World Cup, USA was the defending champion and favorites. Thailand was ranked 34th, and had only ever recorded a single World Cup victory. When the two teams met in the group tie, USA was ruthless!

Alex Morgan, Rose Lavelle, and Lindsey Horan scored for USA in the first half. A ten-goal blitz came in a sensational second 45 minutes. Samantha Mewis made it four, Morgan struck again, and Mewis got her second to make it 6-0 in the 54th minute. More goals from Lavelle, Morgan (she scored five—see pages 36-37), Megan Rapinoe, Mallory Pugh, and Carli Lloyd cranked the final score up to 13!

USA's ruthless performance signaled their confidence in committing to an all-out attack strategy in a bid to win their second World Cup in a row and fourth in total. Thailand crashed out at the group stage, losing all three games and scoring just once.

HIGH-SCORE HALL OF FAME

1. **USA 13-0 THAILAND** **2019**
   Women's World Cup
2. **AUSTRIA 7-5 SWITZERLAND** ... **1954**
   Men's World Cup
3. **GERMANY 11-0 ARGENTINA** **2007**
   Women's World Cup
4. **HUNGARY 10-1 EL SALVADOR** ... **1982**
   Men's World Cup
5. **HUNGARY 8-3 GERMANY** **1954**
   Men's World Cup
6. **BRAZIL 6-5 POLAND** **1938**
   Men's World Cup

Germany's Birgit Prinz completes her hat-trick in the 11–0 goal rout against Argentina in 2007.

USA's Megan Rapinoe is all smiles as she celebrates her goal and makes the score 9-0 in the 79th minute.

DID YOU KNOW?

After the final whistle, a few of the Thailand players were so devastated by their performance that they could not hold back their tears on the field.

THE FINEST FULL-BACK

RECORD APPEARANCES IN WORLD CUP FINALS!

Brazil right-back Cafu makes it into the realm of World Cup greatness by being the only player to play in three World Cup finals—in 1994, 1998, and 2002—and winning soccer's biggest prize twice.

The first of those finals was against Italy—and the only final to end 0–0 after 120 minutes of hard-fought soccer. In the shoot-out, Brazil held their nerve to come through 3–2, giving Cafu his first taste of World Cup glory. Four years later, Brazil met France in the final but was beaten by a classy French side and Cafu had to settle for a runners-up medal.

As captain at the 2002 World Cup, Cafu led his team all the way to the final. The Samba Boys beat Germany 2–0 and he proudly lifted the trophy for a second time. He starred for Brazil until 2006, and announced his retirement after the World Cup. In an international career that spanned more than 15 years, Cafu earned 142 caps—another record for Brazil.

CAFU AT THE WORLD CUP

1994	**3** Games	**3** Wins	**CHAMPION**
1998	**6** Games	**4** Wins	RUNNER-UP
2002	**7** Games	**7** Wins	**CHAMPION**
2006	**4** Games	**3** Wins	QUARTERFINALS

Cafu in action against Ghana in the round of 16 match at the 2006 World Cup.

PENALTY SUPER STOPPERS

RECORD NUMBER OF SAVES IN A SHOOT-OUT!

2006, 2018, 2022
WORLD CUP

Three goalkeepers stand out in World Cup history for their heroic showing in shoot-outs. Ricardo of Portugal and Croatia's Dominik Livaković and Danijel Subašić, each saved three penalties in a single shoot-out competition.

Portuguese powerhouse Ricardo (right) was the first to do this. Facing England in a quarterfinal shoot-out at the 2006 World Cup, he saved spot-kicks from stars including Frank Lampard, and Steven Gerrard to take his team into the semis. Next was Subašić (top left on p.85) in goal for Croatia in a knock-out clash against Denmark in 2018, also making three crucial stops to put his country through.

At the 2022 World Cup, Livaković became Croatia's hero when they defeated Japan. He went to the left, right, and right again to stop Minamino, Mitoma, and Yoshida from scoring their penalties. Usually it's very hard for a keeper to save one or two, but denying three in a single shoot-out is very special!

Ricardo

FIRST SHOOT-OUT

A penalty shoot-out was used at the World Cup for the first time in 1982, when France and Germany were tied 3-3 after extra-time. Towering Germany goalkeeper Harald Schumacher saved penalties by Didier Six and Maxime Bossis to book a place in the final for his country.

DID YOU KNOW?

Livaković (left) also saved a penalty in Croatia's shoot-out win over Brazil at the 2022 World Cup.

FIVE-STAR FEAT

5

GOALS IN A WORLD CUP GAME!

VS. CAMEROON
1994 WORLD CUP

Russia made a poor start at the 1994 World Cup, losing to Brazil and Sweden. Taking on Cameroon in their final group game, Russia went on a goal-scoring fest, mainly thanks to Oleg Salenko's five-star performance.

Wearing the number nine shirt, Salenko showed all of his finishing skills to help beat Cameroon 6-1. His first goal was from a low right-foot shot in the 15th minute and two more in the final four minutes of the first-half gave him a hat-trick. Salenko wasn't finished, though, with efforts in the 72nd and 75th minutes.

The striker's five goals in a single men's game set a new scoring record. His tournamant total was six courtesy of a penalty in the group game against Sweden. It was enough to make him the joint highest scorer in the competition, sharing the honor with. Bulgaria's Hristo Stoichkov.

GOAL GREATS

Salenko grabbed a fabulous five, but the scorer of Cameroon's consolation goal in this game also set a record. When Roger Milla hit the back of the net he became the oldest player to score at a men's World Cup. Milla was 42 years and 39 days old in this historic game.

Oleg Salenko guides the ball past Cameroon keeper Jacques Songo'o for his fifth goal at the 1994 edition—setting a World Cup record.

DID YOU KNOW?

The six strikes Salenko recorded for Russia at the 1994 World Cup were the only goals he scored for his country.

A PERFECT TEN

10 GOALS!
1991 WOMEN'S WORLD CUP

USA striker Michelle Akers became a star at the first Women's World Cup in 1991. She finished with a winner's medal and the Golden Boot prize as top scorer, netting an astonishing ten goals.

Her ten strikes are the most ever scored by a female player at a single World Cup. Her first came in a 5-0 group stage win against Brazil, followed by a double against Japan in her next game. Heading into the knockout stage Akers was ready to boost her goal count even further.

Chinese Taipei were USA's next opponents and Akers smashed in five as they won 7-0. Her match-winning double in the final against Norway (see pages 60-61) meant she reached ten goals and was the hero as the USA became champion. That's a tough record for any striker to beat!

HISTORIC GOAL

On November 19, 1991 in the opening game of the World Cup, China defender Ma Li enjoyed a memorable moment. In the 22nd minute she nodded in a header against Norway to become the first scorer at the tournament. China, which was hosting the World Cup, won the game 4-0 but Norway eventually reached the final.

Michelle Akers-rises for a header during USA's 2-1 final win against Norway in the inaugural 1991 FIFA World Cup staged in China.

DID YOU KNOW?

Throughout all of 1991 Akers scored a huge total of 39 goals in 25 games for USA.

SHARP SHOOTER

FASTEST WORLD CUP HAT-TRICK!

SWITZERLAND VS. ECUADOR
2015 WOMEN'S WORLD CUP

With just 247 seconds between her first and third goals, Switzerland star Fabienne Humm has the proud record of netting the fastest hat-trick in a World Cup. It took her less than five minutes to create history!

The 2015 Women's World Cup in Canada marked Switzerland's first-ever appearance at the competition. The team announced their credentials with a 10–1 defeat of Ecuador in their second group game, which included Humm's astonishing quick-fire triple. She scored in the 47th, 49th, and 52nd minutes as Switzerland doubled their lead to 6-0, stunning fans in Vancouver's BC Place stadium.

Humm's opening goal was a clever right-foot lob over the Ecuador goalkeeper. She then grabbed her second with a close-range header, and completed the hat-trick with an instinctive poke of the ball across the line. Her speedy skills had smashed the previous women's hat-trick record of eight minutes, set by Japan's Mio Otani in 2003.

I BELIEVE
I CAN FLY...

HUNGARY FOR GOALS

The fastest hat-trick at a men's World Cup was achieved by Hungary striker László Kiss. During his team's thumping 10-1 win over El Salvador in 1982, Kiss hit the net in the 69th, 72nd, and 76th minutes. That's seven minutes between the first and third. What's more, Kiss had only come on as a substitute in the 55th minute!

Fabienne Humm basks in the applause after she stuns the crowd with her third goal in under five minutes!

DID YOU KNOW?

In 2022, Humm scored a winner late on in extra-time to help Switzerland beat Wales in a playoff and eventually earn a spot at the 2023 World Cup.

WIN AND WIN AGAIN!

TWO IN A ROW WORLD CUP TRIUMPHS!

Winning the World Cup is incredibly tough, but to win soccer's greatest prize twice in a row is beyond any team's wildest dream. Across the men's and women's editions only four countries have achieved this.

Italy was the first. The team the men's 1934 World Cup, beating Czechoslovakia 2-1 in the final after extra-time, then became champions again in 1938 by seeing off Hungary. Twenty years later, Brazil lifted the World Cup for the first time and repeated the feat again in 1962. In fact, Brazil almost completed the double twice, winning in 1994, but losing the final in 1998. Argentina (1986 winners, 1990 runners-up) and France (2018 winners, 2022 runners-up) have come close, too.

In the women's tournament, only Germany and USA have tasted back-to-back World Cup glory. The Germans were winners in 2003 and 2007, and the Americans in 2015 and 2019. Japan had the chance of doing the double after they were victorious in 2011 but lost the final four years later to USA.

SUPER MARIO

The World Cup record set by Brazil player and coach Mário Zagallo is unequaled in the men's game. He won two tournaments in a row as a player, in 1958 and 1962, and as the coach in 1970. In 1994 he was an assistant coach when his nation became champion, then took Brazil to the 1998 final as coach for a second time.

Brazil star Garrincha crosses the ball past England defender Ray Wilson in the 1962 World Cup quarterfinal game!

DID YOU KNOW?

When Brazil won their third World Cup in 1970, FIFA allowed them to keep the silverware, called the Jules Rimet Trophy. A new cup was created for 1974.

SELL-OUT STADIUM

WOMEN'S WORLD CUP RECORD ATTENDANCE!

1999 WOMEN'S WORLD CUP FINAL
USA VS. **CHINA**

USA won the first Women's World Cup in 1991 and bagged Olympic gold at the 1996 Games. As World Cup hosts and tournament favorites in 1999, they marched to the final, inspiring the home fans to set yet another record.

Team USA took on China in the final showdown on a balmy day in July. The encounter drew 90,185 spectators into the Rose Bowl in Pasadena, California—the highest attendance at a Women's World Cup game. Although the game failed to produce a goal in 120 minutes, the shoot-out had everyone on the edge of their seats, as they watched USA win 5–4 and become two-time world champions.

The carnival atmosphere inside the packed stadium made the final an iconic moment in Women's World Cup history. The world watched as heroes such as Michelle Akers, Mia Hamm, and Carla Overbeck paraded the trophy on the field, and the celebrations marked a new high for women's soccer.

A packed Rose Bowl in California awaits the 1999 Women's World Cup final to kick off.

CHASTAIN CELEBRATES

At the 1999 Women's World Cup final it was Brandi Chastain who scored the decisive spot-kick in the shoot-out. The left-back converted USA's fifth penalty and dropped to her knees in celebration as teammates rushed toward her. The expression of joy and relief was shared by the majority of fans in the stadium!

DID YOU KNOW?

Earlier on this day at the Rose Bowl, Brazil beat Norway in the third-place playoff match.

PERFECT PERFORMER

WORLD CUP GLORY WITHOUT CONCEDING!

2007 WOMEN'S WORLD CUP

If a team's keeper and defense are in top form, supported by hard-working midfielders, and strikers who take their chances, then glory can come in only six games. That's exactly what Germany did at the Women's World Cup in 2007!

The Germans progressed through the whole tournament and lifted the trophy without letting in a single goal. En route they faced Argentina, England, Japan, North Korea, Norway, and lastly Brazil in the final. Germany goalkeeper Nadine Angerer clocked up a whopping 540 minutes of action without conceding a goal!

Angerer faced a big test in the second half of the final when Brazil striker Marta took a penalty. As calm and as ready as ever, Angerer dived to her right to block the kick and keep the score at 1-0. Germany eventually won the final 2-0 and they had their super-strong keeper to thank for the trophy.

DOGGED DEFENSE

In the men's edition, three teams have won the World Cup conceding just two goals in the entire tournament. The first was France in 1998, Italy followed in 2006, and Spain in 2010. Spain did not let in a goal during the entire four-game knockout phase.

Nadine Angerer lifts the trophy for Germany after her flawless performances in 2007.

DID YOU KNOW?

Goalkeeper Angerer played at the 2007 World Cup because of an injury to regular stopper Silke Rottenberg.

THE *GREATLY* BIZARRE

A World Cup would not be complete without the shocks, twists, and surprises that help make it the planet's premier sporting event. As much as fans want to see the top teams and players hit the highs, it's also amazing when the unexpected happens and a unique World Cup moment plays out. This chapter covers the strange and the spectacular moments that have also earned their place in history!

ZIDANE SEES RED

2006 WORLD CUP FINAL
FRANCE VS. ITALY

France legend Zinedine Zidane was the hero in 1998, scoring twice to help beat Brazil in the final. At the 2006 World Cup final, he was in the spotlight for a very different reason! The captain headbutted Italy defender Marco Materazzi in the chest in extra-time and was sent off. France went on to lose the final on penalty kicks. It was an unbelievable end to Zidane's illustrious World Cup career!

REF?!

DID YOU KNOW?

Both Zidane and Materazzi had made a great start in the match by scoring in the first half. After extra-time it was still 1-1.

THE CRYING GAME

2019 WOMEN'S WORLD CUP ROUND OF 16
ENGLAND VS. **CAMEROON**

England were comfortable 3-0 winners over Cameroon in 2019, but the African team was unhappy in this fiery knockout game. The players complained on the field about video assistant referee (VAR) decisions against them and twice refused to restart play in protest. Some of the players were in tears, which forced their coach to step in and convince them to continue playing!

DID YOU KNOW?
England's first goal was from an indirect free-kick inside the penalty box. All 11 Cameroon players were on their goal line to defend it, but Steph Houghton blasted the ball into the net.

NOT FAIR!

I DON'T TRUST VAR!

BASELESS BLAST

1974 WORLD CUP GROUP STAGE
ZAIRE VS. BRAZIL

Zaire, making their debut appearance at a World Cup in 1974, had suffered a 2-0 loss against Scotland and 9-0 against Yugoslavia in the group. They were already 2-0 down to Brazil before being called upon to defend a free-kick. Zaire lined up on the edge of their box but as Brazil decided who would take the free-kick, Zaire's right-back Mwepu Ilunga charged forward and smashed the ball away. All the players were stunned as the referee reached for his yellow card. Ilunga was clearly unhappy about something!

DID YOU KNOW?

Of course Mwepu Ilunga knew it was against the rules to kick the ball away when the oppposition was about to take a free-kick. It was later revealed that he was making a protest about his soccer federation treating the players badly.

IS HE IN OR OUT?

1998 WORLD CUP FINAL
BRAZIL VS. FRANCE

Ronaldo was Brazil's super striker as the team prepared to take on France in the 1998 final. But his name was left out of their team lineup released just before kick-off—allegedly because of a mystery illness. About an hour before the game Ronaldo was surprisingly back on the team, but he played poorly and France ran out 3-0 winners.

DID YOU KNOW?
Ronaldo did not pick up the World Cup in 1998, but he did win the Golden Ball as the tournament's best player.

ROLL WITH IT?

2018 WORLD CUP GROUP STAGE
IRAN VS. SPAIN

Iran had just seconds left of their group game against Spain. Trailing 1-0, Milad Mohammadi had the ball in his hands as he prepared to take a throw-in to launch it into the box for a final attack. Mohammadi then did a weird forward roll while keeping hold of the ball. He didn't release it, though, and quickly backed up to take a normal throw-in. His attempt at a spectacular roll-and-throw had become a spectacular fail!

KISS MY CLEATS

2007 WOMEN'S WORLD CUP GROUP STAGE
JAPAN VS. **ENGLAND**

England had not qualified for a World Cup competition since 1995, so when the team made it into the 2007 event, the players were eager to make an impression. Star striker Kelly Smith did just that after scoring an equalizer against Japan—she took her shoe off and kissed it. She scored again two minutes later, and this time she took off both shoes and planted a kiss on each!

YOU BEAUTY!

DID YOU KNOW?

Smith was on form at the 2007 Women's World Cup and went on to score another two goals against Argentina to send England into the knock-out phase.

SUÁREZ SAVES THE DAY

2010 WORLD CUP QUARTERFINAL
URUGUAY VS. GHANA

Luis Suárez is one of Uruguay's greatest players, scoring seven goals in 16 World Cup games. Yet, it is something he did with his hands and not his feet that gives the striker his unique standout moment. In 2010, playing against Ghana in a quarterfinal tie, he handled a goal-bound shot on the line from Stephen Appiah in the last seconds of extra-time. Suárez was sent off, Ghana missed the penalty that had been awarded, and then dramatically went out on the sudden-death shoot-out.

FROM HAND TO MOUTH!

The 2014 World Cup was also controversial for Luis Suárez. Playing a final group game against Italy, he clashed with defender Giorgio Chiellini and sunk his teeth into the Italian's shoulder. Uruguay won the match, but Suárez later received a long international ban for the bite.

LUCKLESS LAMPARD

2010 WORLD CUP ROUND OF 16
ENGLAND VS. GERMANY

England star midfielder Frank Lampard scored one of the most famous World Cup goals against Germany in 2010. The problem was the referee and his assistants failed to see that the ball had crossed the line and refused to award the goal.

With England trailing 2-1, the goal could not have come at a better time. Lampard hit a thunderous shot and it struck the crossbar and bounced down a yard behind the line. Goalkeeper Manuel Neuer just picked up the ball and kept playing on as if a goal had not been scored. Lampard could not believe it and England eventually lost 4-1.

DID YOU KNOW?

The incident prompted FIFA to introduce goal-line technology. Nowadays, referees wear a wrist device that alerts them whenever the ball crosses the line.

GERMAN KNOW-HOW

2006 WORLD CUP QUARTERFINAL
GERMANY VS. ARGENTINA

Germany goalkeeper Jens Lehmann used special tactics to beat Argentina in their 2006 World Cup shoot-out. Before the game he had studied which way Argentina's penalty takers were likely to shoot and scribbled his findings on paper. Known as his "cheat sheet," Lehmann kept this in his sock and he consulted it before each penalty.

Lehmann's notes helped him dive the right way to save the spot-kick from Roberto Ayala. As the shoot-out went on, Argentina's Esteban Cambiasso faced a must-score kick. His name wasn't on the list, but Lehmann still looked at the paper and nodded, hoping to convince Cambiasso that he knew which side the shot-taker favored. Lehmann did block the penalty and sent Germany into the semifinal!

DOG'S DAY OUT

1962 WORLD CUP QUARTERFINAL
BRAZIL VS. **ENGLAND**

Playing in a World Cup quarter-final is full of pressure, but imagine how England and Brazil felt when a dog ran onto the field! It happened at the start of the game and the playful pet enjoyed a fun stroll. Brazil players tried to catch it, but finally it was England striker Jimmy Greaves who got down on the grass and grabbed hold of it.

DID YOU KNOW?
As Jimmy Greaves carried the dog away, it got excited and peed on all over his shirt!

GO FETCH!

COMBAT SPORT?

2010 WORLD CUP FINAL SPAIN VS. NETHERLANDS

The 2010 World Cup final kicked off in more ways than one! In the first half, tough-tackling Netherlands midfielder Nigel de Jong kicked Spain's Xabi Alonso in the chest with his studs. De Jong was nowhere near the ball and he floored Alonso with the combat-kick challenge.

Shockingly, the referee only punished De Jong with a yellow card! Thankfully Alonso recovered and played on to help Spain win 1-0 in extra-time. The game wasn't particularly memorable, but fans will never forget how De Jong turned into a wrecking ball in this football match!

THE PRIZED PATE

1998 WORLD CUP FINAL
FRANCE VS. BRAZIL

As host, France was eager to win the 1998 World Cup. To bring the team good luck, defender Laurent Blanc started kissing keeper Fabien Barthez's head before the start of each game. It worked—France lifted its first World Cup trophy!

Although Blanc was suspended for the final against Brazil, he still came onto the field in full uniform before kickoff to kiss Barthez's bald head. France went on to defeat Brazil 3-0.

DID YOU KNOW?

France's goalkeeper Barthez was not only a lucky charm for his side, but he also conceded just two goals in the whole tournament!

CAP TRICK!

2023 WOMEN'S WORLD CUP GROUP STAGE
NETHERLANDS VS. USA

Netherlands playmaker Danielle van de Donk got her sports mixed up during a group game with USA in 2023. She suffered a cut to her head in the second half and the only way van de Donk could play on was to wear a black swimming cap!

The strange head gear was a clever way to stop the flow of blood, but it meant she looked very bizarre on a soccer field. Van de Donk joked about it after the 1-1 draw, however she wasn't laughing when the shiny cap was stretched over her noggin!

ANGIE'S THREE

2015 WOMEN'S WORLD CUP GROUP STAGE
ECUADOR VS. SWITZERLAND

In 2015, Ecuador made its first appearance at the Women's World Cup, but it wasn't the dream debut the team was hoping for. In the three group games, the team shipped in 17 goals!

Most notably, in their 10–1 defeat suffered against Switzerland, Ecuador defender Angie Ponce (right) got her name on the score sheet by converting a penalty. Ponce may have been happy to score the team's only goal in the tournament, but she also struck two own goals in the same match!

POLL AXED

2006 WORLD CUP GROUP STAGE
AUSTRALIA VS. **CROATIA**

Referee Graham Poll's blunder during this group tie in 2006 is perhaps among the most bizarre made by a referee in World Cup history. The English official showed Croatia's Josip Šimunić the yellow card three times—in the 61st, 90th, and 93rd minutes! Poll mistakenly pulled out a yellow card for Šimunić's second bookable offense and only realized his error when he took the yellow out for the third time.

BLOND BRIGADE

1998 WORLD CUP GROUP STAGE
ROMANIA VS TUNISIA

Members of the Romania team that played Tunisia at the 1998 World Cup were eager to create headlines. After winning the first two matches, the whole squad agreed to dye their hair blond for a laugh!

It was really tough to figure out which player was which, and the horror haircuts did not bring good luck because Romania drew this game and then lost to Croatia to crash out of the World Cup. This bunch of blond brothers should never have visited the barbers together!

GOLDEN BOOT OUT!

2002 WORLD CUP ROUND OF 16
KOREA REPUBLIC VS. ITALY

Striker Ahn Jung-hwan's job for South Korea was to score goals at the 2002 World Cup, which his nation co-hosted with Japan. The problem was that his other job was playing for Italian club Perugia. When he scored a shock extra-time golden goal winner to knock Italy out, the Perugia owner was so upset he sacked Jung-hwan and said he'd never play in Italy again!

Jung-hwan had earlier missed a penalty, but he ended the dramatic match as South Korea's hero after scoring a header in the 117th minute. The famous strike meant his career in Italy was over, but it helped take South Korea all the way to the semifinal.